MW01032183

MEDITATIONS

FOR

THE WIDOWED

edited by
Judy Osgood

GILGAL PUBLICATIONS
P.O. Box 3386
Sunriver, OR 97707
(503) 593-8639

Library of Congress Cataloging-in-Publication Data

Meditations for the widowed.

    (Gilgal meditation series)
    1. Widows—Prayer-books and devotions—English.
2. Widowers—Prayer-books and devotions—English.
3. Bereavement—Religious aspects—Christianity—
Meditations.   I. Osgood, Judy.   II. Series.
BV4908.M43   1986   248.8′6   86-15002
ISBN 0-916895-01-7 (pbk.)

Other books in the Gilgal Meditation Series:

MEDITATIONS FOR BEREAVED PARENTS
MEDITATIONS FOR THE DIVORCED
MEDITATIONS FOR THE TERMINALLY ILL
AND THEIR FAMILIES

CONTENTS

IN MEMORY OF OUR MATES

Betty Barber, Dick Baumgardner, Floyd Burns, Carmine Caiazzo, James Childers, Alfred DeStefano, Merrit C. Ervin, Kenneth Gilge, H. Donald Horsley, John V. Jester, Henry G. Kelly, Nicholas Krasnow, Kathryn Marsh, Harold Nelson, Bill O'Boyle, Tim O'Shea, Ruth Price, Michael Roop, Roger Schell, Clifford Stevens, Roy F. Stoddard, Robert Tobey, Jr., Jim Van Zee, C. Donald Vogel, Lawrence Voss, William H. Way, Jerry West, Garth Westcott, Jim White, Shirley Wick, James Albert Williams, Vena Williams, and Walter O. Wilson

ALWAYS WITH WINGS

Some days I am a butterfly
bright and high against the blue —
and some days a moth
drab brown, touching down —
but always . . .
I am with wings.

L. Westcott

It was an important day: the first day of summer, and Father's Day. My husband, Garth, our 9-year-old son, Heath, and I had camped the night before at the base of Mt. Hood with the rest of the climbing party. Now in the earliest bite of the pre-dawn morning, while the climbers readied for their ascent, Heath and I huddled sleepily together and in a whispered conspiracy made plans for the day.

Later, while Heath and I contentedly hiked a lower mountain trail, the climbers struggled toward the summit in deteriorating weather. The conditions on the mountain steadily worsened, and late in the afternoon Garth and four others were killed in a tragic fall.

Since then I have been asked many times if I, too, am a climber. The only mountain I've attempted is this one called "Grief," a treacherous, unpredictable peak which has drained my mental and spiritual resources, as well as my physical strength. Many times, when I thought I had reached the summit, I discovered I still had some distance to go.

During that time of struggle, my first act each morning was to "count my blessings." Yet despite the fact the list was long, I found it difficult to tell God "thank you" for them because I knew he was aware only part of me was grateful.

Then why did I put myself through that each day? Because I was frightened by my own diminishing love of life and I didn't want my son to lose his. My objective became showing Heath the need to appreciate all of life's experiences, holding them close and acknowledging in a positive way both the beauty and the brittleness of life.

In an attempt to accomplish that I came up with a small but powerful prayer which we said each day: "Thank you, Lord, for your gift of life and all the experiences it offers." And out of that struggle came the victory of the summit, for eventually I meant those words.

Again and again, I thank you, Lord, for your gift of life and all the experiences it offers.

Lynda Westcott

OUT OF MY ANGRY GRIEF

"Good" comes to good people and bad people. "Bad" comes to good people and bad people. It rains on the just and the unjust.
James E. Towns, Ph.D.

Cancer took my best friend, companion, lover, and wife from me after 37 years together. I wanted to break the nose of the next person who quoted Romans 8:28 to me. "How can you say God causes all things to work together for good for those who love Him?" My wife was good—and we both loved God.

Her death was not good. It was unjust and painful and a dirty trick, and I questioned a God who would allow this to happen.

Caught off guard one day in the midst of my angry grief, I felt God reach into the wreckage of my life and pick up a handful of bits and pieces. Some were useful, such as mercy and love for others. Those he began to fit into a mold.

The rotting, useless pieces like self-pity and loneliness, He threw aside.

Next He carefully salvaged my water-damaged but repairable emotions, and then He renewed my interest in others who were hurting. It was a slow and painful assembly job requiring friends and family to administer the love to cement my new person of worth.

Knit together by the Master's hand, I began to stand tall before the reflection of what I had become.

He has given me a ministry with the dying and their survivors, and a love for the elderly which led me to become Senior Citizens Pastor of my church.

I was angry at God, but He kept on loving me anyway. I wasn't very lovable, but He stayed by my side. And when the time was right, He used all the broken pieces to mature me so that I might experience a full and rewarding life.

Thank you, Father, for picking up the pieces and making me whole again.

Darrold M. Barber

11

IS LIFE FAIR?

. . . Lo, I am with you alway, even unto the end of the world.
Matthew 28:20 (KJV)

If you think life is fair, you should try to see it as my late husband saw it. He developed serious health problems in his early twenties and had the first of four heart attacks at the age of forty-three. Or you might like to try to look at life through my eyes. I had to bury that wonderful, loving man on his forty-eighth birthday.

No, life isn't fair. We are only kidding ourselves if we try to say that it is.

Yet it is possible to face life knowing that it isn't fair. In fact, I am just beginning to learn that it is even possible to face life when it is almost unbearable.

For months, it seemed far preferable to me to die rather than face a life that did not include my husband. Only recently have I discovered I can continue my life without him.

What made me change my mind? I found the secret of how to face life when it is unfair. It is so simple I almost missed the point entirely. This secret isn't a complicated theological formula, nor does it take many words to explain it. It is best summed up in the simple faith of knowing that God loves us, and that He will take care of us no matter what life brings.

My husband had that kind of faith. I thought mine was better than his. It was based on a complex system of do's and don'ts. His faith was far deeper. He just knew that God would take care of him.

My husband was able to take his faith and use it to help him rise above all the unfair things life handed him. He had to cope with the same negative emotions that plague all of us at times. He was sometimes depressed and sometimes he was angry at life, but he was still able to find joy in living to the day he died.

The joy in his life didn't depend upon circumstances. His joy was in living the best he could with what he had, and in trusting God to take care of everything else. His faith was sufficient for all of his life. Mine wasn't worth much and I had a difficult time learning how to live after he died.

I have learned many lessons from my husband's life, and since his death I've learned others through those who have sustained me on this journey called "grief." One is that God didn't promise to give us special protection if we are good. The promise is that He will be with us no matter what life brings.

There were times when it was difficult for me to feel God's presence because my life seemed shattered. But it was then that I discovered God sends people to care about us, and He sends his love to us through them.

It was a long time after my husband died before I could know joy again, even though that was what he wanted for me. I know it was because he told me that many times before he died.

God wants joy for me also. I know because He tells me so in his Word.

Finally, I have begun to want joy for myself. Sometimes I can only keep it for fleeting moments. Soon I will be able to keep it for all time. True joy doesn't depend on circumstances. It depends upon knowing that God will be with us always, even when life is unfair.

Thank you, God, for the assurance that You will be with us no matter what life brings.

Carol D. White

EACH LITTLE STEP

Cause me to know the way wherein I should walk.
Psalms 143:8 (KJV)

When my husband died I learned the meaning of the word "survivor." I felt like someone whose plane had crashed in an inaccessible location. My companion was dead, but though I was alive, I needed help if I was to make it through that crisis. Without it, my existence was still perilous. But where would I get it when there was no one to rely on but myself?

Although I needed every faculty I possessed just to get through each day, I was in a very real sense paralyzed. Before Dusty's death I was organized and disciplined. Afterwards, immobilized.

It would have been so simple to have remained helpless forever, to have become another victim of that "crash" called grief, but I could not stay that way for I had classes to teach and a child to raise. Like it or not, I had to make some effort to create a new life from our shattered existence.

I began with the parts of my life I could control. Despite the fact I was no longer interested in cooking, I made myself concentrate on proper nutrition because I knew it was important to my well-being, and to my daughter's.

Another step was to take a brisk half-hour walk each day, no matter how I felt, no matter what the weather was.

The third step among those early efforts was to face the mirror and pay attention to my appearance even when the voice within me said, "Why bother?"

Only in retrospect did I realize that each step I decided to take was a little goal I had set for myself. As each was met, others evolved. In time my little goals gave way to bigger ones and eventually I found the things I set out to accomplish were lending meaning to my life again.

My discovery wasn't new or startling. I had just realized one of those truths about life that has to be experienced to be fully appreciated. Setting goals and meeting them gives meaning to our lives. Such is nature's own promise and such was my experience.

Help us to help ourselves, Lord, as we struggle to become more than survivors.

Patricia DeStefano Macari

14

YOU CAN DO IT!

It is of the Lord's mercies that we are not consumed, because his compassions fail not. They are new every morning: great is thy faithfulness.

Lamentations 3:22-23 (KJV)

When I told my brother about the sudden death of my seemingly indestructible husband, I said, "I suppose I'm going to go through a stage of anger about Don's dying and leaving me alone."

"Just because the books say you will feel anger and guilt and depression doesn't mean you have to," he replied.

Although we forget much of what is said to us at such a time, his words stuck with me and became a guideline for many of the situations I had to face. There was no anger, but there were times of guilt. I even felt guilty just because I was positive about death!

I had pictured myself as falling completely apart if I were left without Don because he handled the family finances, he did the grocery shopping, he ran errands, he prepared some meals and washed the dishes (his retirement gift to me), and he wrote letters and planned trips.

And that's not all. When I was timid about accepting a new challenge, he was my cheerleader, urging me on with a strong and forceful, "You can do it!"

Now when business matters threaten to swamp or upset me, I hear, "You can do it" in my heart. Then I settle down and work things out myself, or seek expert help.

When unexpected and overwhelming tears come as I listen to music, watch a play, read a book, hear a familiar phrase, or see something beautiful which reminds me of Don, I am able to turn those tears into smiles as I rejoice in what we had to share. I can do it! I can still enjoy the things we loved.

Having lived for almost forty-two years with Don, who reflected Christ in the way he spoke and acted, I had learned beyond my knowing the lessons I needed to survive without his presence. My husband's death was the ultimate test of all he had taught me and I've discovered he was right. I can do it!

Thank you, Father, for the lessons we learn from those we love.

Edna M. Vogel

A GREAT LITTLE PRETENDER

Faith has a much deeper seat in us than doubt, but most men choose to believe their doubts against their faith rather than their faith against their doubts.

George A. Buttrick

My name is Mary Laura Ann Childers and I live in a little town in the northwest corner of Georgia. You might call me a country philosopher because I like to have a bumper sticker on my car that tells the world what I'm thinking. The one that's on it now says, "Life got tougher, but my faith got stronger."

In a way that summarizes what has happened to me in recent years. The first tough blow was the sudden, unexpected death of my husband on December 11, 1981. The second was the loss of my right leg in an automobile accident in May of 1983.

I spent a year in the hospital after that happened and had to learn to walk all over again, but I'm coping with that loss because of some important things I learned the year before. At the top of that list of lessons is the fact that our problems are God's problems and He will help us with them if we admit the way we feel and ask for His help.

After James died I played a game of make-believe and told myself that his death was God's will, and that everything was all right. I was a great little pretender who kept a stiff upper lip, held my chin up high, and acted like everything was o.k., but I wasn't being honest with God or myself.

It took me some time to realize that I was really angry because I'd lost my husband, and because I was going to have to be without a mate for a long, long time.

When I did figure out what I was doing, it surprised me that I wasn't being completely honest with God. After I admitted that to Him, and to myself, I found some healing in my heart that hadn't been there before. Furthermore, my relationship with God improved and I began to think of Him as my friend.

If I could share just one bit of advice with all the widowed people in the world, it would be this: "Learn to be honest and open in your prayers, and just tell God all your feelings because He knows them anyway."

And I might add, He understands because He's suffered too.

Thank you, Father, for loving us even when we can't admit exactly how we feel.

Mary Laura Ann Childers

BIG BOYS DO CRY

People are lonely because they build walls instead of bridges.
Joseph F. Newton

A friend asked me if men cry when they are alone and lonely. I told her that I do. I'm also fortunate enough to have a few friends who let me cry with them when I need to. They're special people who don't build a wall between us by saying, "Stop," or "Big boys don't cry."

I'm a big boy—and I cry.

It isn't just when I feel loneliness that I need to let the tears flow. It's when I'm most aware that Betty isn't there anymore to tell all those things within me that are crowding to be released. When I have a really good day; when something exciting has happened to a friend; or even when my favorite team wins the world series, I need to bounce that off somebody.

I walk through the door after work at night, exploding with the news I have to share. But the house is empty and quiet; it has no ears to hear, no heart to care. Who shall I tell? I could tell God, but He already knows. So, sometimes, I cry.

When those special friends share my tears, they comfort me. They give me their gift of an open door, a loving heart, a willing ear to listen when I need to talk.

Now, I, in turn am learning to listen to others, to share their sorrow, and to cry with them.

Thank you, Father, for showing us by example that it's o.k. for men to weep.

Darrold Barber

THE PARADOX OF GIVING

For it is in giving that we receive and it is in dying that we are born to eternal life.

St. Francis of Assisi

On September 27, 1975, at the age of 47, I joined the widows of the world. A new life was about to begin. A new life I neither wanted or felt able to cope with.

My husband, John, had been sick for five years. He had endured numerous hospital stays and two major surgeries. All through his illness I had hope. Hope that he would get well. Hope that he would return to work. Above all, hope that we would have a long life together.

Now hope had turned to hopelessness, despair, fear, loneliness and a sense of utter uselessness.

I knew I must somehow continue with the life that God had given me, but how? I had teenagers to raise and I felt totally devastated.

On the positive side, I felt I had a good relationship with God. We talked to each other a lot. Now I turned to Him for help. I begged Him to open new doors for me, to tell me what I should do.

And He did. He told me to help others who had been widowed, but I didn't like that answer. I was worn out, tired and sick, and I couldn't think about helping anyone when I couldn't even help myself. So I told God to quit bothering me.

And He did—for three months. Then I kept feeling like I had to start something. That's the way He lets me know when He has work for me to do. So reluctantly I said, "O.K., Lord. You lead the way and I'll take it from there."

A few days later I noticed an item on our church bulletin board about a workshop for the widowed. I figured I'd go and help those people instead of starting a program myself. So I went, and after the leaders finished their presentation, I asked where they held their meetings. They just looked at me blankly and said, "What meetings? We don't belong to any group." So much for that idea. I was right back to square one, which was "do it yourself."

Well, not quite. My question prompted another woman in the audience to say, "I know who'll help you get a group started." The man she referred to was Father Ken Czillinger, a priest who has a deep love for those who are grieving.

Then I asked God to let me meet another widow who shared my faith and would help me with this project. Through another stranger I was introduced to Eileen Schell. Her enthusiastic response to my proposal left no doubt in my mind that she was the answer to my prayer.

In April of 1976 the three of us started a support group for widows. Forty-five women showed up for our first meeting. Eight years have passed since then and we are still helping those who are in need.

Through this process of reaching out and sharing God's love for us by helping others, I have been the recipient of many blessings. The most noteworthy of these has been the healing of my own grief. That, of course, is part of our purpose, but it didn't occur to me when I started this group that I'd be helping myself by helping others.

One of the other benefits has been the formation of new friendships. Many of us have joined widowed social groups, taken vacations together, and shared special occasions that have enriched our lives.

Perhaps you could guess from what I said earlier that I wasn't known for being unstintingly brave. However, a healthy dose of courage for facing each new day is one of the blessings I have received. And for me, where once there was hopelessness, now there is hope.

Father, we ask you to give us the courage to reach out to others, so that we may learn for ourselves how it is in giving that we receive.

Therese S. Jester

THE GIFT OF LIFE

The ability to cope with grief depends on yourself, the help you get—and the circumstances.

Rev. Simon Stephens

On March 25, 1983, I gave birth to a healthy 8-pound-baby boy. When I was all settled in my bed after delivery, the nurse drew the privacy curtains open. On the other side of the room was a young couple sharing the joy of their daughter's birth. Their eyes were full of the love for each other that I was longing for so desperately.

"Will your husband be coming soon?" they asked. Somehow I managed a smile. "No, he won't," I said, feeling very alone and totally devoid of the joy that should have filled my being. I pulled the covers up around my face and closed my eyes. Memories began to race across my mind and the voices that brought the news of my husband's death once again rang in my ears.

> *"There was an accident at the factory. Peggy . . .*
> *Carmine's dead. It happened early this morning."*

Silently I cried, "Lord, why do I have to feel this pain over and over again? Why now, Lord?"

When at last I was able to open my eyes, my roommate, Nativity, was looking at me from her bed. "You look like you could use a friend," she said. While I was sleeping someone from my family had mentioned my unusual circumstance within her hearing.

In her compassion she began to ask me about Carmine. Not about his death, but about our life together. I shared with her some of my favorite memories and the pain began to subside. Remembering Carmine like this was bringing light to the dark grief that I had carried for six months.

Our conversation lasted well over an hour and was interrupted only because of the arrival of two nurses and two very hungry newborns. When feeding time was over, Nat turned to me. "Your husband may be gone, but he has given you a gift that no one else could have given you. You have a beautiful son. Take good care of him."

I looked down at Michael and thanked God once again. And then I breathed a second prayer of thanks for the new friend whose listening had eased my pain on the loneliest day of my life; a friend whose compassion helped me feel the presence of God and his love.

Thank you, Father, for the joy a new life brings and for helping me to feel it despite my grief.

Meg Caiazzo

THE COMFORT OF A COLD, WET NOSE

Kindness is a language the dumb can speak and the deaf can hear and understand.

Christian Nestell Bovee

I hadn't even wanted that dog in the first place! My husband insisted I get him to replace the dog that had died recently.

Soon, he was "my dog," a friend and faithful companion; not asking for any more than I was willing to give: a daily meal, a kind word, a warm bed.

But not my bed! No dogs allowed on my bed.

The night after my husband died, I lay there, staring into the darkness, my pillow soppy wet with the unending flow of tears. The bed seemed so big all by myself and I was wondering how long it takes for a good case of "loneliness" to heal when I first felt it move. It was cold and clammy and creeping at a very slow pace into my open hand outside the covers. The solidified jelly-like mass was followed by prickly hairs and just before I screamed, a muffled but familiar whine came from that creature forcing its cold wet nose into my trembling hand.

"Oh, Shawn! What are you doing on my bed?" I threw my arms around his thick, hairy neck and hugged and hugged. God promised that He would not leave us comfortless—and He hadn't.

In the days and months to follow, I came to realize that this dog I hadn't wanted was a gift of love from God. He was the warm fuzzy on my bed every night; a companion always willing, wagging, and available to go for a walk when I needed to get out of the house. Twice, he snapped at me as I wailed loudly and out of control, as if to reprimand me to be strong and of good courage.

Shawn taught me all about love and acceptance and forgiveness. That crazy dog loves me just as I am. And so I've learned to be a warm fuzzy to those around me who are hurting and to approach them gently, loving them just as they are. Like my dog curled up by the warm fire, I just want to be there in case I'm needed.

Thank you, Father, for providing a friend when I felt alone and for the comfort of a cold, wet nose.

Barbara Baumgardner

NO MAGIC WORDS

The world breaks everyone and afterward many are strong at the broken places.

Ernest Hemingway

As an infant, nearly fatal illness.
As a child, divorce of parents and whispering.
As a teenager, long illness with surrender of college
    scholarship, stigma and isolation.
As a woman, death of only child to cancer (son, a college
    senior) and devastation.
Several years later, death of husband to stroke.

That was the last straw. There was nothing left; no one to love; nothing to hope for; no one to laugh with. What kind of life could there be for me, a shell without my fellows—a loser? Why get out of bed?

After two years of little more than bed and tears, a friend's son died in a fall from a second-story window and I went to see her. When I rose to leave, she took me back to her bedroom to show me a certain picture of her son. As we stood together, I felt closer to her than to anyone in a long time and revealed in a single sentence my deep feelings of grief. She quickly responded with, "Oh, you must work through this. I can see the pain in your face."

Her words "work through" nagged at me in the days that followed, but I did not know how to go about it.

Several months later, an optician, struggling to adjust my glasses, sat back on his stool and asked if I had been crying, then why, and said, "You need to talk with someone. Do you know anybody you could visit with?" I mentioned my son's religion professor and added that he was a busy man. "There are many busy people out there" he replied, but your son's teacher might consider it a compliment if you would ask."

More nagging.

I could not bring myself to telephone the professor, but eventually wrote a letter asking his advice and possible referral. He called immediately to say, "Yes, I think you can work through this and be happy again, and I know a person for you to see; in fact, I will make an appointment for you if you like."

Caught off guard, I accepted his proposal, battled fears for two days and met with the counselor, expecting to do my "work" in a month at the most. That time limit was abandoned, however, when I realized my task was not simple, but monumental, and there were no magic words.

I had been holding my deepest feelings inside all my life so that I wouldn't burden others, and they were still there fermenting. So it seemed that I not only needed to express my grief at my husband's death, but also the death of our son 11 years earlier and other losses as well. This I could do only a little at a time and with support.

Fortunately, a self-help group of bereaved parents was organizing and I managed to join them, all strangers, but with a common bond and noble purpose. They showed me it was all right to share my feelings with others.

For the difficult hours, days, nights, I reached deep inside for strength and outward in all directions for someone, something to see me through (a book, telephone call, sermon, lecture, place to talk). On three separate occasions I was ready to quit trying because of the pain, but in each instance a friend took time to visit and encourage me to go on. They did not walk away. Nor did God leave.

And then there were the days that brought fun into my life and gave it meaning again; the days when I rollerskated for the first time in 40 years, with teenaged friends; learned to play pool to fulfill a desire left from my teens; took square dancing lessons; and became a grief resource person.

The holes are there and pain and tears still come, but they no longer possess me. In fact, I have had a certain triumph: emerging as a person. Scarred and flawed, it is true, but a whole person, nevertheless, instead of an empty shell.

Dear Lord, how wondrous it has been to behold the working of your Spirit among the men and women who have helped heal my broken places.

Helen Way

ASKING ONLY HURTS
WHEN YOU DON'T

Because the Lord is my Shepherd, I have everything I need! He lets me rest in the meadow grass and leads me beside the quiet streams. He gives me new strength. He helps me do what honors him the most.
Psalms 23:1-3 (TLB)

Fifteen years ago I was happily married and expecting our sixth child. My husband had just learned that he was to be made an assistant principal in the fall. Our lives seemed as full of promise as the trees outside our windows that were bursting with new growth. But while they were still leafing out he had a mole removed that was diagnosed as a malignant cancer. It metastasized so rapidly that by the time the dead leaves fell from the trees that autumn, his life ended too.

Roger was 37 when he died. I was 34 and our children were 4 months, 3, 5, 7, 8 and 9. After the numbness wore off reality set in and I began to realize the awesome responsibility of those six lives was mine alone. That's when I began to fear the future.

At night I would lie awake wondering how I was going to manage on the small income I had. How would I fit into the business world after being away from it so many years? How was I going to educate the children when it came time for college? How could I afford a car when a new one was needed? And how would the boys grow up emotionally stable without a father-male image?

These questions plagued me, but I kept them inside where they gnawed at me day after day. At times I longed to discuss them with someone, but I really had no one to talk to and there were no support groups then for the widowed.

Eventually the stress I was under led to depression and then to extreme exhaustion. All that gained me was a bed in the hospital and another set of problems because the children were afraid I was going to die too.

I knew that I had to get well and get my household in order, but I didn't know how or where to start. "Please, Father," I prayed, "show me the way." And He did.

Not long after my hospital stay a religious friend, Sr. Josetta, urged me to get involved in the charismatic movement. Through it I learned to trust completely in Christ, and I began to realize that God never gives us more than we can endure. I began to feel good about myself knowing the Lord entrusted those six lives to my care, and I was filled with a sense of peace that filtered out through the children. For the first time since Roger died, order came into our lives.

How did I manage the bills? Well, I didn't do it all alone. St. Vincent de Paul helped me pay the utilities and took care of the kids' dental visits. After my youngest child started school, a friend found me a job. When we needed a car for transportation, I sold a piece of property and made enough profit to buy one.

The Big Brother Program provided male companionship for the boys, and all of the children were able to continue their education with the help of government grants. This year we had our first wedding. My daughter married a doctor and he picked up the expenses for that special day.

All is well in my home. The children and I have managed and they are well adjusted, compassionate individuals, concerned with the needs of others. We have come a long way, a very long way indeed since I learned that I don't have to fight my battles all alone.

Heavenly Father, thank you for the love and support of others that has enabled us to function as a healthy, happy family.

Eileen Schell

THINK OF ME WHEN YOU'RE HAPPY

Happiness isn't something you experience; it's something you remember.

Oscar Levant

There are times when the past calls to me, and I am drawn to yesterday as irresistibly as a child to a cookie jar. I know the delights that await me there, the sweetness inside, and I also know the dangers of getting caught. Yet sometimes the urge is too great to resist and I find myself lost in time gone by.

It seems much nicer there. I know security from loving arms that enfold me when I turn from the present. I know exactly what happened at that precise time, and what was to come in the next moment. There are no unexpected surprises in the land of memories.

However, I can only stay there a short time. A long visit can distort what should remain untouched and true, and discourage the making of new memories. It can also result in sadness and despair.

It's so easy for me to think of my love in moments when I'm sad. But during my short trips to the past, I realize again why I loved him so much. I feel his enormous gift for love, I see his head thrown back in laughter, and watch his eyes twinkle with happiness.

I leave these memories untouched, uninterrupted, and do not disturb them with even a hint of grief. When I return to my world of reality, I think of him when I'm happy and I'm smiling, for the very thought of him demands laughter, not tears.

Lord, help me to always remember your promise that those who weep now, shall laugh.

Linda Taylor Williams

AND GOD CREATED NEIGHBORS

For the whole law is fulfilled in one word, "You shall love your neighbor as yourself."

Galatians 5:14 (RSV)

If you asked me what I thought God created on the eighth day, I'd have to say "neighbors." Without mine—well, I just don't know where I'd be without mine. Let me tell you what I mean.

On a snowy day in February of 1981, Bill, my husband of 37 years, the brave soldier I married during World War II, the man I hoped would grow old with me, was killed by a drunken driver.

Although Bill's work frequently took him out of town, we talked to each other every night. We had a pact. He called one night; I called the next. I was reading the evening paper, waiting for the time to call him, when our doorbell rang. I opened it to find our pastor, close friends, two policemen and my neighbors standing on the porch. When the police couldn't locate me to tell me what had happened, they knocked on my neighbor's door and they, in turn, notified others to rally support for me.

Sometimes I think those people have ESP. Other times I know they do. It was uncanny how they would call again and again on those days when I was in the pits. "How about going out to dinner?" they'd ask. That was their way of discovering what kind of mood I was in at the moment.

If I didn't want to go out, they came over and sat and talked with me. And they listened. Oh, how those people listened, as I repeated over and over again all those things the bereaved have to talk about to accept what has happened.

The neat thing was, they didn't come because they were prompted by my family or anyone else. They came out of a sincere concern for my well being. And you know what? They're still coming! They even deliver a hot meal to my door if I'm sick.

These days people frequently ask me what they can do to help the bereaved. I can talk on that subject for hours, or I can sum my thoughts up in a few simple words: "Be a good neighbor," I tell them, "no matter how far away you live."

Thank you, Father, for the neighbors who show us by their actions how much You love us.

Gladys O'Boyle

SOMETIMES A CHANGE IS NEEDED

Rejoice in your hope, be patient in tribulation, be constant in prayer.
Romans 12:12 (RSV)

Going to church on Sunday was as natural as breathing to me, but in the weeks following my husband's death I found it increasingly harder to go. We met in church, raised our daughter there, each taught Sunday School classes, and together we sponsored youth groups, attended Bible studies and worshiped there.

My husband was a builder by trade so, in addition to the fact that he was involved in many phases of church leadership and was church treasurer for the last fourteen years of his life, he was often there doing repair jobs too.

Each Sunday I missed my husband more and more. It grew harder to go instead of easier. I would often sit in the back row and cry even though I'd told myself I wasn't going to do that. Tears came easily, I guess, because so many little things reminded me of him—the communion service which was always so meaningful to us, the concrete walks he poured, a partition he built to divide two rooms. Even the financial reports were hard for me to hear because he had been responsible for them.

I was walking in a gray area of grief where I felt no one else understood. And while I was trying to avoid it, I'm sure I let some self-pity creep in.

A dear widowed friend of mine accepted the challenge of taking her husband's place as elder when he died. While I was glad for her, for some reason I couldn't seem to do anything like that myself. I determined to keep trying though, to keep my eyes on Jesus and search the Bible for more of God's words for me.

While doing that reading, the words in the scripture quoted above came to mean a lot to me. "Rejoice in your hope" — because of Jesus, I knew we would be together again in eternity.

"Be patient in tribulation" — I felt the Lord had taught me much about being patient while my husband suffered those nine months with cancer, but I sensed He had more to teach me.

"Be constant in prayer" was like a directive to me so I began to devote more time to that activity. I prayed for my church, for it's work and outreach, and even for the people individually.

Gradually I was able to sit through the worship service without weeping. But there was still a restlessness in me.

After months of growing in prayer and asking for God's direction for me, I began to feel a sense of wanting to visit other churches. Eventually I found one I was deeply drawn to, and now I'm a member there.

My advice to anyone who feels they need to make such a change, would be to do it carefully and prayerfully, taking plenty of time. I waited several years and visited the new church for eight months before making a commitment. I still love the former church and it's people where I belonged for 37 years. And I cherish the memories we three had there as a family, but I had to make a whole new start.

I have found healing of spirit and blessings and work to do in my new church home, particularly in prayer work. And as I've learned more how to cope with my own loss, I've been able to pray and help others in their grief, especially those who have been widowed.

Father God, thank you for showing me that there are many places where I can worship and serve you.

Betty C. Stevens

WHEN DREAMS ARE THWARTED

Be it ever so humble, there's no place like home.
John Howard Payne

As a young bride I dreamed of a home of my own, but it wasn't until my husband, Roy, and I had been married over 25 years that that dream became a reality.

The house we bought sat on an oversized corner lot and, in addition, we purchased the vacant lot next to it which gave us a huge yard and an enormous amount of yard work. But we loved it. Roy and the grand-children had a great time cutting the grass with his riding mower, and I lavished a lot of care on our roses and strawberries.

It didn't seem like we had lived in our home any time at all before Roy experienced a series of medical problems that greatly reduced his strength. For many years after that we struggled to maintain our house and yard as we had when he was well, but eventually it got to the point where we had to sell our place because we couldn't keep up with the work. Although I would have preferred to buy a condominium, it looked like the best alternative for us would be a mobile home.

We began searching for a new one only to discover that wasn't an option because there were no vacant rental spaces in our area. That meant we had to buy a used one that was already on a lot, if we wanted to live in a mobile home court, or none at all.

At first our search was discouraging, but eventually we found one both of us really liked. It was less than a year old and in very good condition. I saw myself cooking on that beautiful, fancy stove with the built-in grill and said, "I can be happy here."

Roy agreed, so we wrote an earnest money check and started packing. Unfortunately, the sale fell through because the owners couldn't get the financing they needed to move out. Not only were we terribly disappointed, we had to hurriedly renew our search as we had sold our home in the meantime and couldn't stay there much longer.

After a great deal of looking we decided on the mobile home I live in now. It is smaller than we wanted, but the location is great. Our court is out in the country where the air is clear and the nights are quiet, yet it is still within walking distance of a bus line, a grocery store, and a church.

I was apprehensive about the move, but it didn't take me long to discover that worrying about it was a waste of energy. Everyone in the court was nice and friendly. They could see that Roy was sick and many of them offered to help me.

Within 24 hours of the time we moved in, Pastor McAdams, from that nearby church, stopped by with his wife, Mary, to get acquainted and invite us to their services. Later, a woman from their congregation, who is also a neighbor, seconded their invitation and told us that the people there were very loving and caring.

She wasn't exaggerating either. The very first time we walked through those doors we felt as though we belonged. When the services were over we left with a warm and happy feeling and a sure sense that God was alive and working in that little church.

A few months later Roy died. I'm not sure how I would have coped if it hadn't been for the continual support of that little band of people who loved me with God's love. By their words and their deeds they have shown me that God loves me and they have helped me feel good about myself.

While Roy and I had belonged to a church for years, we had never been active members. However, it wasn't until we found this congregation that we realized what we had been missing.

Once in a while, particularly when the closets seem too small, I still wish we had gotten that first mobile home we tried to buy. But everytime I bring the subject up, my daughter reminds me that it wasn't in a quiet safe location like this court is and says, "I wouldn't feel good about you being there."

Then she adds, "I think God knew you needed to be here, Mom. He also knew these people would make you feel good when they hugged you and that they'd support you when you were alone."

And you know what, I think my girl's right. This house wasn't what I wanted, but it's close to the church I needed, and all the closets in the world couldn't hold the sense of peace that I've found there.

Thank you, precious Lord, for leading me where I wouldn't have gone myself.

Mable Stoddard

I WILL BE WITH YOU

Fear thou not; for I am with thee: be not dismayed; for I am thy God: I will strengthen thee; yea, I will help thee.
Isaiah 41:10 (KJV)

When my wife died I knew all the questions grieving people ask. I learned them during the years I served as a pastor and heard my parishioners voice them one by one. Still, that didn't keep me from asking them myself or from traveling the same emotional road each of them had trod.

The first thing that struck me was sorrow for myself and the enormity of my loss. I asked, "Why me?" and said, "I should have gone first." My ego was surrounded by ego; north, south, east and west.

Then fears crept in. Fear of making it alone—there were so many adjustments to be made. Fears of my health holding out— would family and friends stay by for one as they had for two? Financial fear—my wife was a good manager: can I make ends meet? Social fear too—when the amenities have been done by church people will I be left to "make it" without support?

Guilt, too, settled in and I caught myself repeating its well-worn lines, "If only I had done this . . . " or "if I hadn't done that."

Was it easier for me to cope because I expected sorrow and fears and guilt? Yes, to the extent that I knew they were a normal part of grief. No, because knowing didn't make battling them any easier.

What really helped was an experience I had had some years before when it looked like I wouldn't survive a serious illness. I was terribly worried then because I still had a 16-year-old daughter at home and my resources were quite limited.

Seeking help and direction, I took a vacation and spent five days in constant and earnest prayer. Finally, an answer came: *Go ahead; live your life one day at a time and I will be with you as life opens up to you and you go along.*

As I said, knowing the questions didn't make my grief any easier, but knowing that God would be with me day by day did.

Thank you, Father, for being with us day by day through the good times and the tough times in our lives.

Rev. Hampton Price

CONSIDER THE GIRAFFE

And if I laugh at any mortal thing, 'Tis that I may not weep.
George Gordon, Lord Byron

I had always skated over life's rough spots with humor. When things went wrong I could laugh or cry, and I usually chose to laugh.

We can be almost sure that God has a sense of humor. Otherwise, why would He have created the giraffe, the zebra, and the fiddler crab? And since we are made in His image, isn't it conceivable that He instilled in us the ability to see humor in life's situations and in ourselves.

My husband, Tim, and I had always laughed at life's adversities together, but during the last year of his life that was beyond us. There was nothing funny about the fact that he was dying and we, who loved each other so much, would soon be separated by death.

After the funeral I was sure I would never laugh again; that humor, my armor against the world, had been buried along with Tim. I found nothing to laugh about when the car refused to start, when mice invaded my home, when the rusty bottom fell out of the hot water heater. Life had become a grim battle of survival.

But as the grief subsided, I realized that neither God nor Tim would want me to drag through cheerless days indefinitely; that I owed it to myself and those surrounding me to try to bring back the joy of living. Laughter had served me well in the past. Perhaps it would see me through the terrible transition that widowed people must make.

So I began to pray about it: "Please, God, give me a joyous heart. If I can joke and laugh once again, I can face most anything with your help."

And in time the ability to see life's humor and to laugh heartily did return. When I think of Tim today, it's his smile that I remember, and when I think of God I see him designing the giraffe, and the zebra, and the fiddler crab.

Dear Heavenly Father, thank you for bringing back the laughter.

Nancy O'Shea

CHAPTER THREE

My days have passed, far otherwise than I had planned . . .
Job 17:11 (TJB)

I suppose everyone who loses their mate of many years questions why marriage should end with the death of one partner. Hadn't we become one? Was that why I felt like half a person?

What I wanted was to have ended life as we lived it—together. But what I wanted was not to be, and I like millions who have come before me and millions who will come after, was faced with the task of learning to live the rest of my life alone. I fought that reality at first and tried to live by just doing the things we had done together, but that was too painful.

Then one day it came to me that my life was made up of chapters. The first covered the years when I was single. Then there was marriage. And now a new one had begun.

Once I accepted that fact, I began to look forward to the next chapters in my book. I didn't know what was going to happen, but I realized that they were mine to write. And so I began to lead my life in such a way that I would enjoy what was written on those pages. There was no reason for my life to be dull when I could make it exciting, so I took control and made things happen.

My first step was to transfer to a closer church because I wanted more frequent fellowship than a half-hour drive allowed. A new hobby, genealogy, brought a whole new dimension to my life, including new cousins.

I took a creative writing course at a local college and was thrilled to find acceptance among students from all walks of life, most of whom were young. Their perspectives added a nice balance to my volunteer job as program chairman of the retirement complex where I live.

When Walter died I thought it was the end of everything, but I was wrong. My life isn't over. A new chapter has begun with new challenges and new opportunities.

Thank you, Lord, for helping me to see that the end of one chapter is the beginning of another.

Jane G. Wilson

SECURITY RESTORED

Fear not . . . for your Maker is your husband.
Isaiah 54:4-5 (RSV)

Several months after my husband died the verses quoted above helped me discover an incredible secret. Let me explain.

The year 1975 was very difficult for me. By then I had been severely ill and house confined for seven years. That was a nightmare in itself, and it didn't seem possible or ever occur to me that further tragedy could befall me, at least, not while I was totally incapacitated. A trauma of that magnitude happened only to someone like Job, didn't it?

But in my case, the incredible did happen. My husband's own illness and job insecurity brought on such deep depression and delusions that in desperation he took his own life. Suddenly I was more afraid than ever.

That was ten years ago. I still don't like living alone, but I am no longer the frightened, helpless woman I was then.

What made the difference? What enabled me to cope?

I read a magazine article that reinforced an idea I'd encountered several times before. It encouraged me to think of God as my husband and trust him as I did my mate.

Obviously it didn't mean that I would fix his dinner and iron his clothes, the way I had for Harold, but I could talk everything over with God, ask Him for advice, and trust Him to fill my needs. Those were all things that I knew I could do and to a great extent I did do, but when I began to think of God as my unseen partner, things began to change in my life.

Slowly my fears subsided, slowly my loneliness abated, and slowly my health improved. And as those things happened, I realized faith chases fear away.

That's the incredible secret I mentioned, the one that has enabled me to do what I once thought was impossible, and that I think is far too good to keep.

Thank you, Lord, for the assurance that with You by our side, we are never alone.

Marilyn J. Nelson

THAT "LOOK"

I sought my God,
My God eluded me.
I sought my soul, my soul I could not see.
I sought my brother one day,
*   and suddenly I found all three.*
                        Father Carey Landry

There is no mistaking that "look." It is stamped on the face of each newly bereaved person I meet. Yet while it is obvious to me now, I failed to recognize it until the day I saw it on my own face in the mirror. It appeared after my husband died quite suddenly in 1981. Since then I have discovered that death gives us, if we look for it and allow it, the ability to see beyond our own pain and recognize it in the lives of others. I learned that from an elderly man on an airplane.

It happened at Eastertime when I was traveling with my children. The older gentleman who sat next to me had that "look" on his face. We chatted quietly and he spoke to my son in a grandfatherly way for the longest time. Finally, I asked him if his wife had died recently. He looked surprised and shocked by my question, but answered "yes" and asked how I knew. I said it was written on his face.

He looked at my child then and asked if his father was dead. After I nodded "yes" he began to talk about his wife, telling me how she died painfully and slowly. Then he asked about my loss.

We shared. No age barrier was evident at all. It was a warm and wonderful experience, and the knowledge I acquired by the end of that flight was remarkable. Suddenly I was seeing with eyes that had not seen before and hearing with ears that had not heard. Sitting there, listening to another's pain, I realized that all my life I had been concerned about myself and not my fellow man. And I also realized that when I found my sister or my brother, I found myself as well.

Thank you, Father, for the gifts that come from our pain.

                        Nancy Voss

THAT'S NOT BREAD; THAT'S CAKE!

Action may not always bring happiness; but there is no happiness without action.

Benjamin Disraeli

I'm not sure if it's the eating or the aroma that inspired me to bake zucchini bread so often. It certainly was tasty, but the blending of spices, nuts, and dates seemed to linger in the air a little longer than most of the baking I did.

Coming in the door my husband would hesitate, sniff upward and smile. I could always count on the same comment at the dinner table. "I just don't understand why you call that bread," he would say. "That's not bread; that's cake!"

After he died, I realized that baking goodies was one of the many things I did for him that I truly enjoyed doing. Now there was no one to make that ritualistic comment; no one to stand at the back door and breathe in the scrumptious scents from the oven; no one to tease me about "fattening him up."

In an attempt to satisfy that emptiness within me, I made cookies, pies and even my favorite zucchini bread specialty and delivered them to unsuspecting friends and neighbors. That was enjoyable, but somehow not the same.

Then one day it happened. For some reason I was so hungry I was ravenous. A survey of the refrigerator and pantry yielded nothing that would satisfy. I was consumed with a desire for zucchini bread, moist and nutty and sweet scented. Finally yielding to my craving, I reached for the bowl and mixer.

I not only baked two loaves, I ate several slices while it was still hot. Then I purposely went outside and returned, inhaling deeply, savoring the fragrance that filled every nook and cranny. "That's not bread; that's cake!" I laughed aloud.

That was the day I knew I was beginning to heal.

Thank you, Heavenly Father, for the healing power of special memories.

Barbara Baumgardner

FOLLOWING A NEW ROAD

Know this, that he that is a friend to himself is a friend to all men.
Seneca

I had to acknowledge and accept the fact that I would always be lonely before I could handle my loneliness. That there would never again be a glance across the room holding within it remembered fun, shared joys or sorrows, or understanding of the present moment that went beyond words. That there would be no arm across my shoulder promising support, comfort, or tenderness. Only then could I realize it was my responsibility to develop and grow, or retreat and wither.

My choice was to reach out, and when I did I found friends at church, at a senior center, and in my apartment complex. Yet after fifteen years of widowhood, when I am full of the need to talk of my day, I still experience acute loneliness when I open my door and only silence meets me. It is then that I telephone a friend to find they are as much in need to share their day as I. We make plans to meet or talk again and I put this on my calendar. A calendar gives purpose to a day.

I felt a recurring loneliness when I stretched out a cold foot in bed and there was no warm foot to meet it. So I bought an electric blanket and its cozy warmth insures sleep most nights. But, if I do wake up, I reach for pad and pencil and list all the things I should do. Then I list what I'd like to do. New ideas often challenge me in the morning.

One scrawl said, "Do something you've never done." Searching for that "something," I looked at the typewriter on which I had hunted and pecked for years. Then I bought *Touch Typing In Ten Easy Lessons*. Well, maybe, but I'm better than I was four months ago! Another time I took pencil drawing at a senior center and looked at the world from a different perspective. That gave me new self-confidence!

Time alone threatens, so I turn to books. Books to laugh with when I eat my solitary meals. Books to grow with in discovering new worlds. Mysteries for suspense and certainty of solutions. Books to argue with. Old friends re-discovered on my own shelves. Books for spiritual food.

Thus I fill my days with possibilities and give thanks to God who has led me to them.

Dear God, help me to keep growing and to reach out and discover anew the wonders in this life you are giving to me.

Betty Kelly

BECOMING WHOLE; BECOMING ME

For I know the plans I have for you, says the Lord. They are plans for good and not for evil, to give you a future and a hope. In those days when you pray, I will listen. You will find me when you seek me, if you look for me in earnest.

Jeremiah 29:11-13 (TLB)

Grief has been a paradox for me. I have mourned my husband, Nick, with my entire wounded being and suffered the pain of his absence from my life at its very center. The aloneness of widowhood has engulfed me.

Living since Nick has died has taken every degree of mental, physical and spiritual strength I could summon up. At times I felt totally stripped of everything except a paralyzing pain that filled and entombed me. Over and over again, a voice within me has pleadingly cried, "Let me out." Helpless, I have cried out to my God for His help. And therein lies the paradox.

Even in the midst of my most awful pain I was aware that He tenderly comes to me and reveals Himself in simple, ordinary ways like the caring touch of another, a listening heart, an encouraging smile that says, "I believe in you."

That awareness has created a peaceful stillness within me. Softly, something began to stir at the very center of my being and it has freely flowed on in a steady positive rhythm.

Now my heart is flooded with song. The words echo and re-echo telling me the Father knows me by name and is calling me to new life. His love unbinds and sets me free.

Ever so gently His hand moves across the days of my life and He points me in the direction I should go. Little by little I let go of the past and try not to look back. Instead I embrace each new day with enthusiasm and an open heart. I believe and trust in God's plans for my welfare and I am excited about my future.

I know I shall never be the same, but I shall not be less than who I am. Within me lies the full potential to be the "me" God continually invites me to be. "Yes" is my response to each of God's invitations to continue to blossom and grow. I freely choose life, and in the midst of my aloneness I am whole and I am ME, loving and loved.

Dear Father, thank you for calling me forth to new life

Mary Ann Krasnow

OVERLOAD

Everyone can master a grief but he that has it.
William Shakespeare

It was a dark day when I read a sentence in a book on the processes of the body that linked stress and certain illnesses. Dark because it confirmed my suspicion and tightened the hold of guilt on me concerning the deaths of my son and husband. A stroke had taken my husband, and cancer had claimed our son.

Illnesses had plagued me through most of my life until the underlying cause was finally identified and surgery performed. That brought improved physical health for me, but my emotional state worsened. It became abundantly clear to me that if I had not been their wife and mother, my husband and son would be alive and well—that I had killed them.

This I could not live with, so I began a frenzied search for medical information that would refute it, but found instead what I read as an accusation. I then turned to the grief literature and the helping community, hoping to find a person with some authority who would take my guilt away, but it seemed to be immovable.

In print or in person, I was told to claim it, give it to God, and leave it forever. I was scolded for using time and energy on the past that could not be changed. I was reminded of God's forgiveness and the need for me to forgive myself, and told that I might be making myself too important. There is no doubt in my mind that many of those who gave advice were well-intentioned, but nothing I did, with or without prayer, seemed to make a difference.

A slight change came when a respected counsellor said in a workshop on guilt that for some persons "there is no complete absolution and they must go on functioning in a disabled way." "That's me," I thought. He also said that the person with the guilt is the only one who can blow the candle out, but that I could not do.

Much, much later, in an evening talk group, I acknowledged for the first time my great struggle with guilt. I intended to be brief, but once started, I could not seem to stop the flow. In a moment of panic, I realized that I needed an ending and heard myself say, "I did not do it; I couldn't have; I loved them dearly. IT HAPPENED, and that is how it stands. The winds of release swept over me and my candle blew out.

Thank you, Lord, for helping me to realize that sometimes the experts are wrong.

Helen Way

A MOTHER'S DAY CELEBRATION

*In times of afflication we commonly meet with the sweetest experiences
of the love of God.*
                    John Bunyan

Shortly after my wife died I found it necessary to go out of state for
temporary employment. During that time I was only able to come home
on weekends.

One Saturday a neighbor called and asked me to babysit for his children
early the next morning which was Mother's Day. He wanted to take his
wife out to breakfast. To tell you the truth, I resented the request because
I had so little time at home with my own family, but I couldn't say "no."

When I arrived at his home I found the whole family dressed up and
ready to go. Excitedly, they told me, "You are a mommy too, and we're
taking you out to breakfast for Mother's Day."

Their thoughtfulness brought tears to my eyes.

Mother's Day had always been a special, honored day in our home; a
day when "Mama" had breakfast brought to her in bed. The children did
the housework and we all took our special lady out to dinner. I thought
that maybe, if I didn't remind my children of the day, they would forget
it and I could bear the hurt by myself.

After my "babysitting job" I hurried home and the children and I went to
church as usual. Afterwards, on the way to the car, one of them said,
"This is Mother's Day; aren't we going out to dinner?"

"Yes, yes," all five of them cried in agreement. "Why should we stop
going out for dinner on Mother's Day just because Mommy died?" They
hadn't forgotten their Mother, or the fact that I was trying to fill her shoes.

I'd had a tough time trying to be both mom and dad to my kids since I'd
lost my wife, and there were a lot of times when I wondered if I was doing
an adequate job. But that day I felt good about my dual role. My children
let me know they appreciated my efforts, and I felt God had honored me
in a very special way.

Thank you, God, for giving fathers the ability to be mothers when they
need to be.

                    Dave Williams

I'M NOT CRAZY: JUST BEREAVED

Some days I think I'm going to go insane thinking about it, and you can't not think about it, ever.

Judy Osgood

For 17 days I stood by his bed and watched his body deteriorate from a healthy athletic man to a wasted shadow, incapable of even taking a breath on his own. "He's going to die" my head would say, and my heart would scream, "Liar!"

Finally came the night when his heart beat so hard the bed shook, and his body arched in convulsions. I held his hand to my cheek and whispered, "Please God, if he can't be well, take him now." Two hours later my love slipped from my helpless hands into the loving arms of our Heavenly Father. For him, the hurt was over; for me, it was only beginning.

With the funeral over, the mourners gone, the flowers themselves in a state of death, I began searching for help to put my shattered life back together. I went to the library and checked out every book I could find on being a widow. In several there was a reference to a group called *THEOS*. I called the Crisis Hotline and United Way to find out more about them, but they had never heard of the group. In an area of over five million people, I was alone!

When I had been widowed about six weeks, I saw a notice about a seminar for widows. It was sponsored by a Houston college and was to be led by a minister. I called an acquaintance who had been widowed four weeks, and together we drove 50 miles across Houston traffic, desperately seeking help, only to be sadly disappointed.

The "seminar" for newly widowed attracted about 15 women; all had been widowed from 5-15 years with the exception of Laurie and me. Many had had numerous affairs, some had become alcoholics, most were still under psychiatric care, and some were suicidal. I remember one topic vividly: "What were your sexual feelings when you walked by the casket?" We left as quickly as possible, knowing only that we did not want to follow in the footsteps of those women.

For eight months I struggled alone with my grief. There were times when I thought I was losing my mind, and other times I was sure it was already gone. I couldn't concentrate. I thought I had lost an insurance check for several thousand dollars, only to discover it had never been issued. Sleep was a luxury that eluded me night after night.

One day I read in the paper that *THEOS* was forming a Houston chapter. I again made a long trip across the city at night, this time alone in case it turned out like the last one. The room was packed with women of all ages. A lady named Theresa Marsh stood in front of us and said, "I am not a widow . . . " and I almost turned her off right then.

But Theresa's story was unique. Her son had drowned in the Houston floods the year before, and, seeing her daughter-in-law's grief, she felt compelled to try to help others. She made a plea for help and even now, five years later, I'm still helping.

Theresa guided us for over a year and while I am not as active as I used to be, I still write a monthly article for *THEOS* magazine. That organization gave me a purpose in life. I felt that I had to do something to honor my husband's death, and what better way to do it than to help someone else get through the despair I had known all too well.

With the people at *THEOS*, which I learned is an acronym for They Help Each Other Spiritually, I found people who shared my feelings. I didn't have to put up a front with them. If I felt like crying, I cried. We shared each other's sorrow, and eventually we shared each other's laughter.

For five years now I've also taken calls for the Crisis Hotline. I don't know how many have interrupted my sleep, and I've lost track of the number of times I've reassured the caller that time does help. Occasionally, when the work has left me emotionally drained, I've thought, "no more sad stories; enough is enough!" Yet, Crisis Hotline still has my phone number and I still say that time will help because it's true. And if the saints in Heaven can see what's happening here on Earth, I know my love is cheering me on there as he did when he was here. *THEOS* and its people saved my sanity, and I hope I've passed that love and caring on to someone else.

Thank you, Father, for groups like *THEOS* that give us the courage to go on living and to enjoy life again.

Linda Taylor Williams

THEOS is a national self-help group for young and middle-aged widows and widowers. For more information, write to: THEOS, Suite 410 Office Building, Penn Hills Mall, Pittsburgh, PA 15235.

HOARDING AND HANGING ON

The man who lives by himself and for himself is likely to be corrupted by the company he keeps.

Charles H. Parkhurst

Cleaning out the garage was the hardest part. I didn't mind giving his clothes and shoes and underwear to folks who needed them, but what things would I need to keep from that abundantly supplied garage?

When I finished, the pile outside was small and the garage was still crowded with power tools, hammers, axes, fishing poles, sleeping bags, camping equipment, a set of saw-horses, a backpack, a box of plumbing wrenches, a creeper to get under the car, a vise, nails and screws and buckets of bolts. They were all things I thought I might need.

It's hard enough to lose a husband, friend, and lover after 31 years, but when he died he took with him my carpenter, plumber, electrician, woodsman, appliance repairman, mechanic, and camping companion. Certainly I would have to learn to do those things by myself.

In the three years that followed my garage cleaning endeavors, I used a hammer and one nail to hang a picture. That was all, but the clutter still remained.

One day I stood watching crowds mill around and through the merchandise at a garage sale. What was selling quickly were the wrenches, screwdrivers and fishing equipment. Young family men scrambled for items to do their own plumbing, mechanical work, and appliance repairs.

"Pass them on, honey, you don't need them. They do!" The silent voice within my heart caused me to hang my head in shame. I'd been hoarding and hanging on, unwilling to let go of this part of my husband that would never be used again.

Shortly after that I held my own garage sale and it was a smashing success. Now that space is clean and empty and I've put up curtains at the windows for a feminine touch.

I wasn't just holding onto things; I was also hanging onto what once was. As I see it, my husband was like the stalwart trunk of a tree and I am learning to prune and let go of all the helpful limbs he once provided.

Thank you, Father, for experiences that give me insight into my own behavior.

Barbara Baumgardner

CHERISH THE MEMORIES

We can fall on our faces in despair or use the time on our knees to gain God's strength and then get up, and go on, stronger than before.
Eleanor Tyler Mead

"This better not take long," my husband said, when he checked into the hospital for tests. "I need to start combining in two or three days." But before the week was over, Jim's damaged heart stopped beating.

In our farming and livestock operation we spent most of each day together. I lived my life loving Jim, caring for him and helping him with whatever needed to be done.

The week after he died our crops had to be harvested. Friends, neighbors, and relatives came to help in an overwhelming show of love, but in my heart I resented the fact my husband wasn't running the combine himself. Later, our livestock, machinery, and land were sold, and each sale was another finality that made losing Jim unacceptable to me.

For the next few months I dwelt on the past and brooded over our unfulfilled plans. I hated not having a husband, envied married couples, and blamed God for putting me in this situation.

Then one day I realized what a bitter person I was becoming because I refused to accept what had happened to me and be grateful for what I still had. And I knew that would have made Jim sad, for every day at mealtime he had prayed, "Help us, Lord, to be more thankful for what we have."

What I had left was our beautiful daughter who was a joyous reminder of the love we shared. And I had a storehouse of precious memories from the 13 years of our marriage—a storehouse I could draw nourishment from any time I needed to.

I began to go to the storehouse and found myself smiling as I remembered the work we'd done together, the happy times we'd shared. When the good memories replaced the shattered dreams, I found that I could go on loving him, not in the way I really wanted, but in a new way. And that has sustained me and helped me learn to live again.

Thank you, Lord, for helping me to realize what I have and to be thankful for it.

June Van Zee

HIS FURRY LOVE

. . . All creatures great and small,
. . . The Lord God made them all.

Cecil Francis Alexander

Riley was really Tim's cat. When we got him as a tiny kitten, Tim said, "Well, he's going to live the life of Riley, so we may as well name him Riley." Tim died when Riley was eight years old.

During the days surrounding the funeral, Riley was a frightened shadow that darted in and out between the legs of family and friends to reach his dish.

How do you tell a cat there's been a death in the family? Riley only knew his man was missing, and he displayed his sorrow in various ways. He even took to sleeping in the uncomfortable plastic recliner where he had never slept before unless the man was also in it.

But cats are adaptable creatures, and in time he turned to me, smothering me with his furry love. Through nightmare nights he plastered himself against me, and once when he annoyed me by scratching a flea, I hurled him away in exasperation. But he was back on the bed with the speed of a rocket. He had forgiven me. He had also shamed me. After all, he constituted my immediate family.

There were days I wouldn't have gotten out of bed except for Riley. He was most self-sufficient, but he did need someone to open the door and dish up the cat food. I learned he also needed someone to brush his fur and dust him with flea powder once a week, and there were occasional trips to the vet. Riley's needs forced me to think of something besides myself and my grief.

Soon he trained me to cut delectable leftovers into tiny pieces and set them down for him. And he needed someone to talk to, so eventually we engaged in conversation, often about Tim and how much we missed him. I catered to his whims, as Tim had done, and I have been well paid for my efforts.

He loves me with an unconditional love. He is a warm living presence that needs me. I can tell him my innermost thoughts, and he blinks large yellow eyes and seems to understand. It is comforting in the night to reach out and pat the large furry lump on the bed. There is no doubt that Riley has helped me through the most difficult period of my life. I hope I have helped him too.

Thank you, dear Heavenly Father, for the small creatures you send to brighten our lives for a little while.

Nancy O'Shea

TOO PROUD TO CRY

The first step in dealing with weeping is to realize the fact that it is an emotion and that it is God's way of helping us to relieve inner pressure.
James E. Towns, Ph.D.

During my husband, Donald's, illness, I felt like I had to stay strong for his sake. When death came, I was standing by his bedside, holding his hand and fighting back the tears. The nurse asked me to leave the room and I obediently did so; trembling and numb.

Until then I had always thought I could face anything, but as I walked the corridors I found myself feeling weak and disoriented. In a daze I wondered, "Where should I go? What should I do?"

Suddenly I felt alone; so terribly alone that the impact of that emotion hit me with the force of a physical blow and I literally staggered to a doorway and held on.

"Is something wrong?" a weak voice asked.

I looked up and saw a tiny elderly lady who was sitting in a chair in her room. Her frail form was wrapped in a heavy robe and her deep sunken eyes seemed to fill her whole face.

Nodding my head I told her that I had just lost my husband.

"Come in and sit for a while," she said. "I seldom have company and no one will disturb you here."

And so I sat, breathing deep sighs until I regained my strength. As I rose to leave I thanked her for letting me rest a moment. "That's quite alright," she answered, and then added in almost pleading tones, "Maybe after all this is over you'll come back to see me."

After the funeral was over and despair had set in, I thought of her and I did go back to visit. We talked of other things at first and then, finally, of the day I stumbled into her room. I told her then of my determination not to cry.

"To cry is not a sign of weakness," she said. "I cry often." As she talked on about the purpose and value of tears, I realized that I had been too proud to cry and silently those healing drops began to flow.

Thank you, Father, for the sweet release we feel when tears wash away our tensions and ease our fears.

Dorothy Horsley

THE FATHER'S BLANKETS

There is no pit so deep but what His love is deeper still.
Corrie ten Boom

For a year and a half after my husband was murdered, I sat. Not just sitting, but stuck, motionless. Dead, but breathing. My life was centered then around endless pots of coffee, cartons of cigarettes and a kitchen table constantly wet from tears. Now and then I would tend to a child who screamed so loudly that he couldn't be ignored, but I really didn't see anything or anybody except the images that danced in my head.

My mind was filled with technicolor pictures of Mike's distorted body before and after death, as well as repeated thoughts of what must have happened that night. He was on a trip and wouldn't give his seventy dollars to the people who wanted it.

Somehow, murder seemed socially unacceptable. Good people don't really get murdered; things like that only happen on television, or far away to people we don't know and probably wouldn't care to know.

Even the word is so shocking I hoped no one would ask me how he died.

Loneliness, anger, isolation! A struggle? NO! A bloody war just to reach where the naturally-widowed person begins.

Time passes slowly, but as it does the difficult images fade and our perception of reality changes.

Now I can see clearly what I only suspected occasionally in the beginning. There are blankets wrapped around this family. They are the Father's blankets, warm and fuzzy, disguised as caring, supportive people. The ones always closest to us, trying, and the ones He has sent in our direction since. I've managed to find these blankets in each place I've crawled or walked: in church, on street corners, in police departments, supermarkets, family gatherings, shopping malls, bowling alleys and even in the strangers who might be knocking at my door.

I thank God for allowing me to finally see clearer His people for what they are. Without them I'm certain I would still be sitting at my kitchen table, buried in the past. They try to comfort. No matter how the words come out, they are trying to comfort and because they are there the anger and isolation lessens.

After three and a half years some find the way to ask questions. Probably the toughest one to answer is, "How do you do it?" Tough, because it stirs doubts as to whether we really are doing it. But the bottom line is, we are surviving . . . with God. Now, before, and always. When the doubts and fears creep in, I work hard to remember I am not alone. I close my eyes and see blankets, soft and warm.

Lord, thank you for the human blankets that wrap us in your love.

Judy Roop

TRUST

Many will see and fear, and put their trust in the Lord. Blessed is the man who makes the Lord his trust.

Psalms 40:3-4 (RSV)

Shortly after I received a phone call informing me my husband had collapsed while playing racquetball, I read the words quoted above. Though I stared blindly at my open Bible, the word "trust" seemed to jump off the page at me. It was the only word I saw.

Sitting there, realizing I was a helpless child with no control over the situation, I also realized with sudden clarity the power of God. Not only did He have the power to let Bob live or die, but He also had the power to help me handle whatever would happen.

That night Bob's life on earth ended. I was 27 at the time and pregnant with our first child. In the weeks and months since my husband's death I have asked God "Why?" too many times to count.

"Why did it happen now with our baby on the way?" "Why did my mate have to die?" "Why?" "Why?" "Why?" He was such a good husband and would have been a great father.

I didn't get any direct answers to my questions, but each time I asked I was reminded of the night Bob died and the word "trust." It was as though I had to learn to trust God all over again because suddenly something happened in my life that made no sense to me.

Ultimately I came to realize that trust is an integral part of faith and without it faith really isn't complete. My pastor explained it by giving me this example: I see a chair and believe that it will support my weight if I sit on it. That is faith. Trust is when I actually sit on it. I needed to believe not only that God was there, but that He would hold me up.

Through my suffering I have come to know the comfort God can bring. I can't honestly say that all of the "whys" have disappeared, but I believe God's word and trust His plan to be perfect.

Thank you, Father, for answering all my questions with one simple word.

Maureen Tobey

A MOVING EXPERIENCE

It is difficult to say what is impossible, for the dream of yesterday is the hope of today and the reality of tomorrow.
Robert H. Goddard

One of the wisest bits of counsel I received after my husband died was, "Don't do anything drastic for a year." That meant don't quit your job, don't get rid of too many possessions, and don't sell and leave the family home.

After the loss of a mate it's natural to feel that our life is over. A year or so later, we discover that it was only his or her life that ended. Then as the cloudiness of the mind disappears, we can decide if the house is too big, too expensive, or holds too many depressing memories. If so, it's time to have a moving experience.

For a long time I had wanted to return to the place of my childhood, a small town in Oregon, lush with tall pines, scraggly junipers and so many lakes you wouldn't believe it. My husband and I dreamed of retiring there someday. Could I make this drastic move without him?

Late in August I drove into that town alone and frightened, holding a long hand-written list of requirements clutched against the steering wheel. I had asked God to provide specific answers enabling me to be comfortable with the pending decision, but I wondered if I wasn't being too blunt and specific with Him.

I had asked for doors to open in my profession; for fond childhood memories to be abundant, and I got really specific with the home I wanted to purchase. The list I gave the real-estate man was long and meticulous.

The agent apologized for showing me one house on the way to the one he knew I'd like. The second one was completely in compliance with my list and I bought it.

Memories and employment opportunities emerged with smiling faces, beckoning me to "come home."

Tears obstructed my view of the mountains as I hurriedly drove away to pack and prepare for my move. God had provided answers to specific needs and now I could say good-bye to old friends, vacate the family house, and close the book on a past life. I was going home!

Thank you, God, for providing me with a home here on earth and in eternity.

Barbara Baumgardner

ELDERHOSTEL

If I should not be learning now, when should I be?
Lacydes

This "Noah's Ark Society" that we live in makes a single feel like a fifth wheel. And I suspect that's particularly true for the widowed who have spent years being half of a pair. However, since my husband died I've found an activity for those over 60 that I can attend by myself and thoroughly enjoy. This summertime program, which is sponsored by colleges and universities all across this great land of ours, is called "Elderhostel."

For those of us who were raised during the depression days and couldn't afford to attend college, the Elderhostel experience is a new and marvelous one. Most are held on campus while the regular students are on vacation. Three classes are offered during these one-week sessions and all those attending are required to attend at least two.

Participants sleep in the dorms, eat in the cafeterias, go to class during the day and pursue other activities together during the evenings. And the cost is reasonable.

The first year I went I took Creative Writing and Indian Culture. The second year I served as a hostess for the group and it was my pleasure to brag about our little corner of California to my fellow students. We came from all walks of life. There were retired teachers; an insurance man; a former district attorney; a social worker; several housewives; a nurse; a postal worker; and myself, a secretary. Despite the differences in our backgrounds we were a very congenial group.

Another year I went to an Elderhostel at a small private college in Ohio and took courses on "Our Amish Neighbors," "Handling Stress," and "Gilbert & Sullivan." In the latter course we studied the lives of the men who wrote the operettas, attended a dress rehearsal where we met the cast, went backstage to see the props and the costumes, and then were guests of the theater at the opening night of "The Pirates of Penzance."

I appreciate Elderhostels. They add a lot to my life as a single because I make new friends, learn new things, and am richer for the experience. I am thankful for them.

Thank you, Father, for opening new doors for those of us who are walking through life alone.

Rosella L. Ervin

A MATTER OF PERSPECTIVE

And my God will meet all your needs according to his glorious riches in Christ Jesus.
                                        Philippians 4:19 (NIV)

January eleventh. How would I get through that first anniversary of Ken's death, I wondered. Would I relive that early morning phone call and the dash to the hospital with my son, Den. "Not the respirator again," my heart had cried. "Oh, Lord, please not another coma."

We had lost count of the times Ken had been revived those two months since he had sustained a brain-stem stroke. But now he had been in a private room four days, the tracheostomy had healed shut and he could speak, although he could not swallow or balance.

I think I knew as the doctor walked toward us before I heard, "No pulse. No blood pressure. He's gone."

"It's over! It's over!" I had sobbed on Den's shoulder.

And now almost a year had passed and the grief waves had become less frequent and intense. Still, I dreaded that anniversary day. "Lord, help me over this hurdle," I prayed.

On January eighth Den phoned and said, "Want to go out to dinner with us Wednesday night, Mom? It's payday."

We both knew it was more than "payday," and, of course, I eagerly accepted.

Wednesday morning when I woke I began to pray, "Lord, help me think the right thoughts today," and suddenly a scene flashed into my mind's eye—the same little mini-vision I had the day Ken died. I saw my husband gazing around himself, face radiant, eyes filled with awe, and I knew he was saying, "Wow! Wait till Jeanette sees this."

That night at dinner I told Den and Barb what I had seen. "And," I said, "my predominating emotion this morning was gratitude. Every time I'd think of my hurt, I'd recall his glowing face, and I'd feel happy for him instead of sorry for me."

While that may seen incredible, I think it's just a matter of perspective. When you love someone you want the best for them, and knowing that Ken has it now enabled me to see January eleventh, not as a tragic day, but as a day of triumph.

Father, help us remember that you have ways to help us beyond our wildest dreams.

                                        Jeanette Gilge

A CHOSEN VESSEL

Be aware of me. I can accomplish great things through even one yielded, believing vessel.

Frances J. Roberts

For seven unbearable months I lived in fear and dread after the doctors told me that my husband had a malignant brain tumor and only a few months to live.

My initial reaction wasn't why. It wasn't anger, nor was it rebellion. I simply became almost catatonic with fear. Jerry and I were approaching our twenty-fifth wedding anniversary and after all those years with him, I knew I could not survive without him any more than I could breath under water. Therefore, God would have to heal him.

During this period of agony, Jerry and I met a radiant widow. She had lost two husbands on exactly the same date, in the same kind of accident, nine years apart. I asked no questions, but she told me in a soft, happy voice, "I'm a vessel now . . . available for anything."

I backed away from her and instantly told God, "Don't you ever expect me to be a vessel. Not ever. I am a wife and I must continue to be a wife. I must grow old with Jerry. You need to understand that. I can take my own life if you don't do things my way."

Then one night, after seven months of holding onto Jerry, God spoke to me while I was struggling with fear. He asked, *"Will you trust me as never before? Will you relinquish him to me? I am going to heal him, but it will be with me. It all fits into a plan that you cannot understand. Don't try. I'm bigger than you think. Can you release him yet?"*

In a moment of desperate anguish I told God the impossible, the unthinkable. I said, "Okay, God."

And suddenly, for the first time since we received his diagnosis, I wasn't afraid. Joy seeped back into my frozen heart and I was once again aware of God's love and power. I don't know how such a change could have occurred so quickly, but I do know that when fear is forced out all kinds of victories are possible.

Immediately then I prayed, "God, I want to be a vessel. Use me anyway you chose."

Two months after I released Jerry, he died. Yet the joy that came to me that night remained with me through those final weeks together and it was a feeling that Jerry shared. We called the service we held for him a "homegoing celebration" because he had gone to be with his Lord, and that new life for my beloved husband was cause for rejoicing.

I don't know how it was possible to maintain that spirit, but I think it has something to do with being a vessel—a servant willing to do whatever God asks. The term is one which was frequently used in biblical days. At that time some vessels were golden while others were made of clay, but each was chosen by its owner for a specific purpose.

When someone like myself says, "Lord, make me a vessel," we're really saying that we are willing to reach out and minister to anyone, anywhere. That, I've discovered, is often costly, but there are marvelous benefits. For one thing, I am now living free of fear for the first time in my entire life. In addition, I'm eager to see what each day will bring.

Even without Jerry my life is filled with joy despite the fact I once thought I would never taste it again. In fact, I was so sure of that I had decided to chop down our dogwood tree if it dared to bloom after Jerry died. That's because I saw it as a symbol of new life, and at that point in time I was sure it would be impossible for me to ever rejoice if my husband were to have a new life without me. But when I released him and said, "Lord, make me a vessel," all that changed.

Thank you, Father, for showing me the only way I could experience joy once again was to become a vessel.

Marion Bond West

In her book, The Nevertheless Principle, *Marion Bond West shares more of her experiences and the discoveries she has made since her husband's death.*

THE KEY TO INDEPENDENCE

Trust thyself: every heart vibrates to that iron string.
Ralph Waldo Emerson

"Where do your children live?" asked a new acquaintance a few years ago.

"Boulder, St. Louis, and Minneapolis," I replied, feeling considerable self-pity knowing her grown children all lived near her.

"Wonderful!" came the cherry retort. "You won't bother them, and they won't bother you!"

Stunned at the time, I've now come to realize why she made that comment. Not only am I free to do what I want, but I'm free to discover what I can do.

It took some time for me to realize that I could learn to do things for myself without bothering my family, that I did not need to consult a daughter or son-in-law every time a business or personal problem arose. And, as I look back, developing my independence from them has actually improved our relationship.

Dependence on another is a luxury which many of us lose with widowhood. A key to avoiding over-dependence on those close to us is to become informed and then to trust ourselves. We have to get busy and learn: "Nothing ventured; nothing gained!" We'll make mistakes, of course; but learning from our mistakes will produce successes.

Early in my widowhood, I had to learn to handle business and financial affairs. I took continuing education sessions to at least learn the vocabulary of investments and real estate. Through Powder-Puff Mechanics class I found out what spark plugs are and where the oil and transmission fluids belong, and that has given me confidence when I have to leave my car for repairs.

Recently I had to dispose of the house I grew up in. Before I sold it, I spent eight months studying various aspects of real estate in the area. Finally, after verifying the home had historic restoration potential, I was able to negotiate a price double that estimated by the first real-estate appraiser consulted. Being free from the burden of the house was a relief; but more important, my self confidence ballooned.

So now, to build my ego as well as avoid leaning too heavily on my daughters and their families, I'm researching options and making decisions, yet inviting input from them when circumstances permit. That solution seems to be a good one for us.

Since we all live far apart, we try to gather at a lakeside summer cottage, overlapping visits for a long weekend or two if possible. On such occasions, time and freedom to explore my personal concerns is limited. I try to remember to use those special times instead to find out more about them—about their jobs, their interests, their friends. They too have decisions to make; and their's deserve whatever of wisdom and experience our time together permits me to share. Besides, I don't want to return to my solitude and realize, "Oh dear! I talked about myself so much I didn't learn about them."

Several years ago I heard a sermon called "Aloneness." "We come into this life alone," the minister explained. Then, despite spouse, family, and friends, "We progress through life alone, and we leave alone."

When I am bothered by twinges of self-pity, his message is a comfort, strange as that may seem. For I have known the joys of being a wife and that was good, but I have also learned to walk by myself, and that too is satisfying.

Thank you, dear Lord, for supporting me in difficult times and for helping me to develop my talents to meet the challenges ahead.

Ruth Kivett-Burns

HAVE CAMPER —WILL TRAVEL

In this world there is always danger for those who are afraid of it.
George Bernard Shaw

People were curious or shocked. Some thought I was courageous. Others were sure I'd gone off the deep end as I prepared to take my vacation alone. I knew, of course, that many women never go anyplace because they're afraid to travel by themselves, but I wasn't going to let that attitude keep me housebound.

The estate had been settled, my late husband's business was closed down, and his clothes and tools had been disposed of. That was all finished and I needed to try my wings.

I bought an eight-foot camper to put on the bed of the pickup I'd retained from Dick's construction business. Promising my grown children I would check in "every so often," I set forth with only a tentative itinerary. No reservations had been made so that I would have no deadlines. By 4:00 p.m. every day I settled in an established campground.

My Sheltie dog, Shawn, was my traveling companion. He loved it when I pointed out an elk in Yellowstone National Park and shared my excitement when the herd of antelope scattered on the Wyoming state line.

God's handiwork was vividly displayed in the Tetons, the San Juan Mountains, and in the prickly cactus mingled with delicate wild flowers on an Arizona desert. The Master Artist had prepared the way and I never once doubted my safety. He had always protected me on short trips and I knew He would be my watchman on a long trip too, even alone in an old Ford pickup.

One night as I snuggled into my sleeping bag, the reality of what I was actually doing, alone, unobtrusively crept in. The tears flowed freely yet I felt no sorrow or loneliness.

Probably the most sobering and awakening aspect of my four-week-long trek was that there was no one who needed me those days and no one waiting for me to come home. But that didn't keep me from feeling unmitigated peace that night somewhere, high in the Rocky Mountains. Nor has it kept me from other solitary trips in the years since then.

Thank you, Father, for your protection, day and night, at home and away.

Barbara Baumgardner

THE GRADUATE

To seek the meaning of things and God's will does not spare us either from error or from doubt; nor does it resolve all the mysteries of our destiny . . . nevertheless, it does give a new meaning to our lives.
Dr. Paul Tournier

It's been three years since I said "Good-by" to Betty. She loved life and brought fullness into mine. I still miss her.

But the house isn't all quiet. There's Taffy, the silky sable Cocker Spaniel who came to live with us before Betty died. Taffy cocks her head and folds her front paws while I clean the oven and do my ironing. Those inquisitive, chocolate brown eyes search the path of the vacuum and puzzle over my domestic efforts. I wish I could speak her language and answer all the questions I see in her wrinkled expression.

Betty and I had a lot of questions too and often talked about all the things we would someday ask God. At times our list was so long we were sure it stretched halfway to heaven. The scriptures we read together either fed our needs or left us wondering. In the latter case, we discovered that not having all the answers motivates faith. "We'll just ask God when we see Him," we'd say to each other.

One day, when I was thinking about a Biblical question, it hit me that Betty knows all the answers now because she's with the Lord. No more uncertainties; no more doubts; no more wondering. She has taken her big, long list to the Master Instructor. Betty has graduated!

I smiled when I found myself thinking how neat it is that she's found the answers we searched for together. And I rejoice that her life is complete.

In my mind I place a cap and gown upon her memory and a diploma in her hand while I still hold the list of questions in mine.

Until my graduation time comes, me and Taffy with the big brown eyes, will keep on questioning . . . and ironing, and vacuuming.

Thank you, Dear God, for the assurance that one day I'll know the answers to my questions too.

Darrold Barber

WHAT MIGHT HAVE BEEN

For of all sad words of tongue or pen,
The saddest are these: "It might have been!"
John Greenleaf Whittier

It seems to me that those of us who have been widowed could easily waste a lifetime dwelling on what might have been. No matter what our age, we still think about the children we never had, the anniversaries we never shared, the trips we never took. We know we're in that never-never land when we find ourselves making statements like, "he would have retired in another six months," or "we always wanted to build our own house."

Those are what I call "double-edged yearnings." They're precious because we shared those dreams with our loved one, but dangerous because, if we dwell on them, we can mourn away our life instead of living it.

Nothing can change "what might have been" into reality. The ending will be the same no matter how many times our mind replays those dreams. If we are to heal, we have to give them up.

If your mate, like mine, was a vital person who loved life and lived it to the fullest, you may be destroying what he or she held most precious. Ten years from now, even tomorrow, will you look back on today and remember with contentment that you lived it to the fullest, or will you say, "If only . . . it might have been!"

God, please help me release what might have been to enable myself to look for what still may be.

Linda Taylor Williams

THAT AWFUL QUESTION

Goodnight, Mrs. Calabash, wherever you are.
Jimmy Durante

Durante's ringing curtain line was a tribute to his deceased wife, Jeanne. He so named her after they had driven through the small town of Calabash on their way to California. The name amused them both, and thereafter he fondly called her Mrs. Calabash.

After 22 years of marriage, Jeanne died. Jimmy didn't marry again for 17 years, so it's safe to assume he didn't intend to remarry unless he found just the right person.

After being widowed myself for six years, the question I find hardest to answer is, "Why don't you get married again?" I am often tempted to snap, "Because no one *ever* asked me," but that's not the real reason. The real reason sounds so trite.

I believe it was Pearl Buck who said, after her husband's death, that their marriage was a jewel set in eternity. While I realize there is a tendency among the widowed to idolize the deceased, I was married to an exceptional man, and I think we had an exceptional marriage. Yes, a jewel set in eternity.

Shortly after Tim died, I was engaged in conversation with another widow. "I got married again," she confided, "but this one's been sick ever since I got him." Just as though she had gone to a pet shop and gotten another puppy!

I have found only one advantage to being a widow, but it is an important one—independence. I cherish the freedom to come and go as I like, whenever I like, to do or not to do. I'd joyfully give up my liberty if the jewel could be re-set, but I refuse to trade it off for a marriage of convenience.

Tim was a gift from above, and it's unrealistic to believe God has another gift of equal worth in store for me. If, in the years to come, He chooses to bless me again with the "just right" person, as He obviously did Durante, I may change my mind. But like Jimmy, I am in no hurry.

So the next time someone asks me the dreaded question, I think I'll just say, "Maybe someday," and let it go at that.

Meanwhile, goodnight, Tim, wherever you are.

Thank you, God, for the good years you gave us and the happy memories they generate.

Nancy O'Shea

CRISIS AND FAITH

It is only when you have been burned to ashes that you completely find God. Then when everything in you seems to have been extinguished, a new little flame is somehow lighted, which grows and grows and can never be put out. That flame is God.
Walter Russell Bowie

It seems to me that grief's survivors are characterized by a unique combination of vulnerability and strength. Despite nature's healing process, the grief experience leaves one irrevocably altered.

Grief invaded my existence when, nearly three years ago, I became a widow. Although I have been favored with new-found love and have recently remarried, I continue to acknowledge grief as the wisest and most thorough of teachers.

In the desolation of grief's wasteland, I learned the meaning of the Biblical revelation that, as the heavens are above the earth, so are the ways of God above our ways. The barren terrain of loss became the testing ground of my faith.

Time ceased for me as a result of the total emptiness that replaced my once meaningful existence. Prayer became an impossibility and God's presence, even His existence, was not worth the questioning as, practically speaking, it could not alter the pain that enveloped me.

In the absence of faith, I turned to my own faculties for survival. Combining the need to give a voice to my torment with a propensity for writing, I indulged myself as never before. Day after day, week upon week, month following month, I labored to express, as factually as possible, my experience of grief. The result was a journal which has subsequently been published as *Interlude Of Widowhood*.

More than any other tool of survival, this writing advanced the healing process. Specifically, the forging of my chapter on rediscovering the spirit produced the most tangible, almost miraculous, results. Putting into words the seemingly simple statement that, even in my most desperate moments, I knew deep within that God had not abandoned me, released a flood of tears that surpassed all the oceans wept in preceding months.

Writing this chapter was also a milestone in my life. Prior to doing it, putting my thoughts on paper was laborious. So were my efforts to rebuild my life. The remaining chapters, however, seemed to write themselves as my words began to lift my own heart. I could feel my spirit prepare to soar, though how or where I did not know.

The fact that I have since embarked upon a new life and love in no way depreciates the wisdom born in me before any new love came to me, for it is a wisdom imparted by grief.

Certainties and answers are not mine for the seeking; neither is God. Illusive, He abides so deeply within me that His presence is revealed only when the terrors of the interior darkness have been penetrated. Searching for the demons of doubt inhabiting that darkness, my own person is rediscovered, and in the courage which I never knew I possessed, He reigns.

Paradoxically, I fear future losses as only one who has fallen into grief's abyss could fear descent; meanwhile I am strong as never before in the knowledge that, while it is useless to seek a miracle to restore life, I already possess whatever miracles are needed to survive death.

Though we would never seek the wisdom that only grief imparts, Father, nevertheless we thank you for it.

Patricia DeStefano Macari

EASTER SUNDAY AND OVEN STEW

*The weather-cock on the church spire, though made of iron, would soon
be broken by the storm-wind if it . . . did not understand the noble art
of turning to every wind.*

                                        Heinrich Heine

It kinda knocks the pins out from under a guy when death comes,
unsuspected and unannounced. She hadn't been sick or pale or even
tired. Yet, so quickly she was gone.

I asked myself, "Is this for real? Can this be happening to me?"

Yes, it was real, and God is real, and He's never failed me in all the many
years I've known Him, but I still asked, "Why did she have to die, God?"

Our two grown daughters were visiting from out of town when it
happened. It was Easter Sunday, a day that had always been special to
me because I knew that our Lord had risen from the dead to walk again
among men on that first Easter. Victory over death was cause to rejoice!
But this Easter was different.

On this Easter my wife, Kathryn, died and instead of victory, I felt defeat
and devastation. Immersed in grief, I could not rejoice that because of
Christ's resurrection she too had a new life to lead. I just kept thinking,
"she won't be coming back to me."

One daughter sent her family home after the funeral. She stayed to teach
me how to live alone. During that time she gave me simple recipes that
I could do all by myself. Some were for one person, others would feed
company too. The one I liked best was for an "oven stew" that just got
better and better. And, incidentally, so did Easter Sunday.

After the shock wore off and the pain of early grief subsided, I stopped
asking "Why?" Since then Easter seems to have grown more special with
each passing year. I guess that's because the one nearest and dearest to
me has experienced the victory over death that God bought for all of us
with his Son's life, and to me, that's the best reason of all for rejoicing.

Thank you, Dear God, for loving us enough to pay such an enormous
price for our lives.

                                        Paul Marsh

A SEASON OF SUICIDE

To every thing there is a season, and a time to every purpose under the heaven: A time to be born, and a time to die . . .
Ecclesiastes 3:1-2a (KJV)

"He took his own life" sounds like something he was entitled to do. After all, it was his life to do with as he wished, wasn't it? Well, wasn't it?

When the news came, we numbly whispered impromptu answers as people insensitively questioned his motive. "Why hadn't he wanted to live? Was he depressed? A financial crisis—marriage problems?" And then the inevitable question, "Was I, his wife, to blame?"

Was I? Was I responsible for his life—and his death?

I tried to deny it happened. Bearing the grief of death was a full load by itself. I tried to avoid those friends who knew how he died. Their eyes questioned my bewildered existence.

As the survivor of my marriage, I hungered to know the truth; to ask the questions that could no longer be answered. Thus my journey through a season of self-examination became a tug-of-war between my life and his death.

It took time to recall circumstances that might have influenced my husband's self destruction. As I dissected and analyzed each turbulent situation, I asked God to forgive me for my error or mishandling of the event, and then I forgave myself, knowing that there was no way I could change the past.

Painfully, tearfully, and slowly I examined our seasons together. When I finished, I was free and forgiven and no longer floundering in self-inflicted guilt.

No, I was not responsible for his life; therefore was not responsible for his death. It was his choice to escape from what he thought was an intolerable time.

As the seasons come and go, I find "a time to weep and a time to laugh, a time to mourn and a time to dance." (Ecclesiastes 3:4)

"He hath made everything beautiful in his time." (Ecclesiastes 11a)

Thank you, Father in heaven, for the dark times and the light, and for the changes in the seasons and ourselves that enable us to heal and become the people you would have us be.

Barbara Baumgardner

TWICE WIDOWED

We walk by faith, not by sight.

II Corinthians 5:7 (RSV)

"Twice widowed," murmured my cousin, gently pressing my hands in greeting. I nodded, tears threatening, "Yes—but—I'm so grateful for the days Floyd and I had together. They were marvelous."

Prior to that second marriage, I had been a widow for eighteen years. I survived those lonely nights, years of stretching pennies, risking decisions all alone. Immersing myself in a young family, a teaching career, and a few hobbies that forced me to have social contacts, I found a satisfactory niche and learned to enjoy independence. I built an identity. A postal clerk, an intern, even a young policewoman in a neighboring town would stop me with, "You're Mrs. Kivett! Remember me? I was in your class . . . "

Suggestions of remarriage had no appeal. I told myself to avoid risk of another upheaval and loss. Only rarely did I date.

Early in widowhood I had declined an invitation because I knew I could never care for the man who extended it. My teenage daughter had counseled: "If you accept, you know he'll ask you out again; and it'll just be harder to decline later."

Midway in my widowhood, a former college romance bloomed again. However, the sudden heart attack and death of my friend halted hopes. For a time I was devastated anew.

Then, more recently, a former acquaintance, a widower, re-entered my life with a whirlwind courtship. And I rediscovered love. But should I remarry? And what could the future hold for us? Did I dare risk the agony of losing love again? Should I disrupt my secure life pattern and risk another funeral, another readjustment? Floyd was nine years older than I; besides, women live longer than men.

I followed my heart, and now I am twice-widowed. Instead of agony and regrets, however, I feel so thankful for the days Floyd and I shared. Though our time was short, just over two years, that second marriage enlarged me and my horizons and brought such joy and happiness to my life. I've learned that love once shared and the spirit it engenders is never truly lost. Instead, love expands our selves and opens doors closed before.

Thank you, Lord, for giving me the faith and the courage to open my heart to another love.

Ruth Kivett-Burns

THE OLD BOOK OF LIFE

Destiny is no matter of chance. It is a matter of choice: It is not a thing to be waited for, it is a thing to be achieved.
William Jennings Bryan

I hugged the book against my breast, savoring the adventure I had just completed. An hour slipped past as I relived the story as if it were my own.

While reading the book, I had loved each person in it; they had become my own intimate family for a few short hours.

Now the book was finished and it was time to put it on the shelf, but it wasn't easy to let go. The leading character had died and I had grieved and wept with the family and friends. Their loss was my loss.

I wanted to read the book over and over again, but somehow realized it would not be the same. There was no way I could relive that story now that I knew its outcome. Instead I would have to go to the library and check out another book.

How often we who have been widowed try to continue to live the same old story and to act out our lives on the same stage after the death of a loved one. In reality our life, or story, cannot go on the same as before. We have been made new creatures; the stage has changed. We are approaching a new adventure, but first we must put our old life on the shelf. Then we can begin our own new story.

Could this volume have more unforeseen excitement, more satisfying service, more joyful events, and more interchange of love than the book just finished?

There is no way to know until "the old book of life" is lovingly placed on the shelf and the new one begun.

Heavenly Father, thank you for another chance at living a life where I am free to make a choice in my destiny.

Barbara Baumgardner

A LITTLE PRIVATE BOOK

In so far as this record was a defense against total collapse, a safety valve, it has done some good.

C. S. Lewis

I started a journal about two weeks before Tim died, believing I would record a miracle. The last entry was written on the fourth anniversary of his death. Instead of recording a miracle, my journal became a chronicle of suffering, death, and grief, and yet I'm not sorry I kept a record of those traumatic events. With a mind frozen with fear, how could I otherwise remember that near the end I prayed for his death, as it was his best option? That forgotten truth somehow helps me to accept reality.

But most of all, I'm grateful that I wrote about grief. There are thoughts one speaks only to God and a little private book, and while we tend to forget what we tell God, we can go back through a written record and see how far we have come.

C S. Lewis, in keeping his journal, discovered that grief is not a state, but a process, and that is the value of putting thoughts on paper—one can look back and see that progress is being made.

I didn't write in the little blue book every day, but it was comforting to see it on the night table and know it was there, like God was there, whenever I needed a friend.

On the first anniversary of Tim's death I wrote: "Oh, don't think it's over! I'm too heartsick to even pray . . . " At two years I said: "Looking back to last year, I am better." The third year I wrote: I picked the first gardenia of the year this morning. The seasons change, and life goes on."

And on the fourth anniversary: "This must be the outer limits of grief . . . I rarely cry anymore . . . I only hope he knew how much I loved him." The next day I put the journal away.

Occasionally now I take it out of the drawer and flip through the pages: "Deep melancholy remains . . . will I ever be happy again? Morning and night, round and round, life has become like a lonely dance."

Did I really write those words? It's hard to remember that I was once that desolate. With the help of God and the little blue book, I am sane again!

Thank you, Lord, for my love of the written word which has sustained me through many dark days.

Nancy O'Shea

ETERNAL PORTRAITS

May our Lord Jesus Christ himself and God our Father, who loved us and by his grace gave us eternal encouragement and good hope, encourage and strengthen you in every good deed and word.
2 Thessalonians 2:16 (NIV)

For most of us in this nursing home, life is not easy. We must fight off the feelings of despair and hopelessness that seem so overwhelming, refusing to believe that we have nothing more to look forward to. To survive, we must cling to our vision of eternity, and that inevitable reunion with our precious loved ones already gone to be with the Father.

It's been 23 years since I lost my lovely wife, Shirley, but I see her clearly every time I look into the beautiful picture of a forest that hangs over my bed. An artist painted the picture for us during an outing in the mountains, so many years ago. Those tall, majestic trees, the autumn leaves, and the country road represent a very real place with vivid memories.

Absorbed in the painting, I see my wife walking in those trees, just ahead of me. I can hear the birds singing, and they seem to be greeting Shirley as she walks along so gracefully. No words are spoken, but I gather her hand in mine as the leaves float and twist about us in the breeze. Her soft hair is blown about her shoulders, but she doesn't mind. Like the leaves, she appears to be a part of the autumn foilage. Oh how wonderful to hold her again.

Looking into her eyes, I know I will never forget her. My tears begin to drop to the group, but at that moment of pain the Lord appears to help us. We both have faith. We shared the love of God. Our future is guaranteed! My vision ends as Shirley, I and the Lord turn and walk down that country road to our final home.

Lord, I thank you for our beautiful past, but most importantly, for guaranteeing our perfect future.

Robert E. Wick

Please send me the following books:

_____copies of **MEDITATIONS FOR THE WIDOWED** @ $5.95 each = $_____

_____copies of **MEDITATIONS FOR BEREAVED PARENTS** @ $5.95 each = $_____

_____copies of **MEDITATIONS FOR THE DIVORCED** @ $5.95 each = $_____

_____copies of **MEDITATIONS FOR THE TERMINALLY ILL AND THEIR FAMILIES.** @ $5.95 each = $_____

SUBTOTAL $_____

For orders of 10 or more books, subtract 10%. − $_____

Add $1.25 shipping costs for the first book and .25 cents for each additional book to the same address. + $_____

Add $1.25 for each additional shipping address. + $_____

(Gilgal will include a gift card in each shipment to a separate address.)

TOTAL DUE $_____

Name _____

Address _____

City/State/Zip_____

Gift Address

Name _____

Address _____

City/State/Zip_____

Mail this order form to: Gilgal Publications
P.O. Box 3386
Sunriver, OR 97707